Soul Quest

A HEALING JOURNEY FOR WOMEN OF THE AFRICAN DIASPORA

**WRITTEN BY DENESE SHERVINGTON, M.D., M.P.H.
ART BY BILLIE JEAN PACE, M.D.**

Crown Trade Paperbacks • *New York*

Grateful acknowledgment is made to PolyGram Music Publishing to reprint excerpts from "Redemption Song" by Bob Marley, copyright © 1980 Bob Marley Music, Ltd. and "Three Little Birds" by Bob Marley, copyright © 1977 Bob Marley Music, Ltd. Used by permission. All rights reserved.

Published by Crown Trade Paperbacks, Inc., 201 East 50th Street, New York, New York 10022. Member of the Crown Publishing Group.

Random House, Inc. New York, Toronto, London, Sydney, Auckland

CROWN TRADE PAPERBACKS and colophon are trademarks of Crown Publishers, Inc.

Originally published by Physicians Health Management in 1994.

Printed in Hong Kong.

Library of Congress Cataloging-in Publication Data
is available upon request.

ISBN 0-517-88632-4

10 9 8 7 6 5 4 3 2 1

First Crown Trade Paperbacks Edition

For my daughters, Shanga and Iman
For all my mothers
For all my sisters in spirit and blood
For all the precious men in my life
Walter, Jack, and Nicks

For Spirit Marlon and all who love him.
"Life is but a journey that we take. We started the journey alone and eventually finish it alone when we die. I feel like time is ticking away. In this journey of life, our own lives will be involved with good friends and bad friends. But it is all but a journey, which we must take."

—Marlon Depass, 10/13/73–1/13/92

To all the owners of the first publication of Soul Quest: *Thank you for believing.*
Thank you, Lynn, for holding my hands while Adrienne gently shouted, "Push." Thank you both for believing and making this expanded publication possible!

—Denese Shervington

CONTENTS

PREFACE · 4

MOVEMENT 1. **IN THE BEGINNING** · 11

MOVEMENT 2. **DAWN** · 19

MOVEMENT 3. **THE VALLEY OF THE SHADOW OF LIFE** · 27

MOVEMENT 4. **FIRE DANCE** · 33

MOVEMENT 5. **THE HEALING WATERS** · 41

MOVEMENT 6. **THE SEA OF LOVE** · 49

MOVEMENT 7. **SONGS UP HIGH** · 55

MOVEMENT 8. **THE CRYSTAL TEMPLE BY THE RIVER** · 61

MOVEMENT 9. **SOUL FLIGHT** · 67

EPILOGUE · 72

RESOURCES · 77

FURTHER READING · 78

INDEX · 79

PREFACE

My soul feels heavy
It is burdened with the weight of my people.
Just as the cocoon wraps itself around the butterfly-in-waiting
So too the chains of slavery wrap around the heart of my people
They cannot see their beauty, so they cannot feel their wings.
I will soar high among them, so that they can hear me sing
And as their spirits stir, they will hear the heavens ring
And rise, and fly high, Sweet butterflies of spring.

Dear Reader,

Over the past several years in my work as a psychiatrist, I have listened to hundreds of African American women tell their stories of pain. Even though the plot, setting, and props are different for each story, the theme is usually the same. We struggle and search for self-validation in lives bombarded with the injustices of oppression. In response to these stories, I decided to create a process by which we women of the African diaspora could reclaim our worth. Oppression offers us no mirrors that reflect our beauty within. Instead, it weakens and disconnects us from the threads that connect us to the harmony of the universe, the natural order, the ebb and flow of life.

I wanted to create a work deeply rooted in the spirit because we are a people descended from a culture that revered spirit as the connection to the universe in all its mysterious wonder.

The actualization of my creative process began with the following dream:

I am in an airplane en route to Washington, D.C. The principal of my daughters' elementary school is the flight attendant; he appears as a woman. I get off the plane confused about how and why I have made the trip. In trying to make my way to Customs, I keep getting lost. Every route I take ends up taking me nowhere. I begin to descend an escalator, at the bottom of which I see a frightening-looking man whom I fear will hurt me. I try to get away but he snatches me. I smell his stench and see his dirt. Somehow I get away and see my husband awaiting me. He reprimands me for always doing things incorrectly. Try as I might, I can't get him to stop blaming me.

As I began to analyze the dream symbol and images, I realized that this was a dream of transformation. I was beginning a new journey, one in which I was besieged by chaos, the feminine principle. In order to find my way, I first had to face the stench of my aggression, the masculine principle. This energy for so long had been my modus operandi. Beginning the journey of transformation required returning to my feminine soul, just as the principal attending the plane had changed into a woman.

As I drove to work that morning after the dream, this book became alive. All my life I had felt a strong desire to write. During high school, I had always found a way to add a literature course to my science curriculum. Even though I showed a very strong interest in and aptitude for literature, I was not encouraged to pursue a writing career. I was gifted in the sciences, and a career in them allowed me more potential for working my way out of poverty than did pursuing a career in the arts. For years, too, I had equated being an author with writing novels, a task I felt I was not talented enough to master. That morning of my dream, it occurred to me that the fulfillment of my writing desires lay in bringing forth that which came spontaneously from within me—imaginal journeys of the spirit. These imaginal discourses, as I have called them in *Soul Quest,* are visualization exercises that attempt to capture our cultural symbols and connect them to their universal archetypes. With that awareness, I felt totally at one with the eternal creativity of the Great Mother Spirit. I wrote in my diary that evening:

Today is the eve of the celebration of the nineteenth birthday of the spirit of Marlon Depass; I know not why he was killed six months ago. However, his transformation to death has intensified and brought real meaning to my quest. In his honor I begin the journey of my real karma—enlightenment of others through spiritual healing. Today begins the material manifestation of Soul Quest, a spiritual journey for the African diaspora. I know not the start or end. I trust that time and space know no boundaries.

Soul Quest is a vehicle for tapping into and harnessing the power that lies within your imaginal realm.

By immersing yourself in each imaginal discourse and allowing your mind to roam free, you will eventually discover the pathway leading to your inner sanctuary of peace. It is upon this inner stage of quietude that the universe will begin to unfold her mysteries. The tension and fear that arise from feeling separated from the source of life will begin to dissipate! You will feel a renewed sense of direction, clarity of vision, and creativity within your soul. The physical and emotional consequences of internalized stress will begin to lessen.

The imaginal discourses in *Soul Quest* are related to the Hindu concept of the chakras. These are force centers in the body through which the energy of life flows. There are seven such centers, each vibrating to a different color:

the root chakra (red) at the base of the spine

the splenic chakra (orange) over the spleen

the umbilical chakra (yellow) at the navel

the heart chakra (green) over the heart

the throat chakra (blue) at the front of the throat

the brow chakra (indigo) in the space between the eyes

the crown chakra (violet) on the top of the head

Similar concepts relating to the connection of the physical self to the invisible forces of the universe appear in the teachings of ancient Egyptians and Native Americans. In the mind-science theories of the Egyptians, humans are connected to the life-force and the rest of nature through the seven souls: *Kha, Ba, Khaba, Akhu, Seb, Putah,* and *Atmu.* Likewise, among the Native American Hopi, *Kopavi* connects the human spirit to the universe.

The healing in *Soul Quest* is based upon the realignment and balancing of these energy centers as we create more balance between the physical matter of the body and the vibrational energy of universal light. The first two movements, "In the Beginning" and "Dawn," are preparatory cleansing steps. The third through ninth movements correspond to the seven chakras, progressing from root to crown. Each movement is magnificently illustrated by my soul-sister Billie Jean. She captured in her paintings exactly what I hoped to capture with my words; she created pictures to my songs.

HOW TO USE SOUL QUEST

The nine movements in *Soul Quest* progress through the lower, middle, and higher phases of healing—physical, mental, and spiritual, respectively. Each movement begins with an imaginal discourse, a poetic visualization. This is then followed by a "Let's Reason" section, a discussion of the meaning and purpose of the discourse. Finally, there is a series of daily introspective exercises designed to complement the lessons of the discourses. These Self-Discovery and Releasing Exercises provide a structured approach to deeper exploration of your personal life.

Begin your *Soul Quest* journey by working your way sequentially from beginning to end. Start each movement by reading the imaginal discourse. As you read each discourse, allow whatever images, thoughts, or feelings that arise to do so uncensored, without judgment. Next, read the "Let's Reason" section. This is intellectual meandering, meant to stimulate and provoke your own thoughts on the issues. Finally, work through the Self-Discovery Exercises, a series of incomplete statements that you need to finish. They are meant to increase your insight into yourself. You will need to keep a journal to record your responses. The Releasing Exercises are a series of psychodramas to help you act out and release your emotions. Do not spend much time deliberating the Releasing Exercises— just do them!

YOUR JOURNAL

The process of keeping a journal is important because it will force you to pay closer attention to your thoughts and feelings. Be as detailed as you can; do not spare the paper. The trees will forgive you! Be creative with your journal; make it uniquely yours. If you prefer oral storytelling, you can choose to create an audio journal—or, if you're really adventurous, a video journal. Whatever format you choose, allow the voice that you have been silencing to speak freely. Listen to her! You will need to reacquaint yourself with her; she is the floor plan of your life. To make meaningful changes in your life, you must know the foundation upon which you add or subtract. If you do not know how the pieces fit together, things could collapse when you try to rearrange them.

Let your journal be a metaphor for where you are right now in your life, be it a fancy notebook or just a simple notepad. There is no right or wrong way to keep a journal. What is most important is your willingness to face the truth, to be honest with yourself. Pay attention if you find yourself resisting the idea of keeping a journal. This could represent a lifelong pattern of shortchanging yourself, of never quite making it to the finish line!

The imaginal discourses in *Soul Quest* can also be used as guides for visualization and meditation. In supportive group settings, the exercises can be shared to enhance interpersonal learning. *Soul Quest* can also serve as a ritual of passage between adulthood and childhood. By sharing *Soul Quest* with your daughters (in blood or spirit), you can pass along the stories of coming of age.

YOUR BODY

To maximize the healing from *Soul Quest*, pay attention to your body; it is the temple of the soul. I strongly recommend a program of physical fitness (e.g., walking, jogging, aerobics, dancing, yoga, martial arts, weight training), in addition to a nutritional program in which you decrease your intake of fats and cholesterol and increase your intake of water, fruits, vegetables, grains, and complex carbohydrates. Avoiding other health-jeopardizing activities such as unsafe or unprotected sex and substance abuse (e.g., tobacco, alcohol, cocaine, narcotics) is also beneficial.

The purpose of *Soul Quest* is to lay a foundation for your ongoing introspection and growth. It is intended for those searching for a deeper meaning to their lives. It is only the beginning, however. The search for balance and contentment is lifelong; it never ends! If at any point you should feel overwhelmed by feelings of sadness, hopelessness, fear, or rage, please seek therapy with a psychiatrist, psychologist, social worker, or licensed counselor. Resources lists professional organizations where you might seek referrals.

It has been repeatedly echoed by the sages that imagination is the forerunner to action. The realization of your true potential in life begins, therefore, with the imagination of its possibility.

Soul Quest is a tribute to our collective spirit, with psalms of rejoicing, celebrating the victory of our spirit set free. Let us make a merry noise! Come sing with me! In the words of the late poet, philosopher, and musician Bob Marley:

> *Old pirates, yes they rob I*
> *Sold I to the merchant ships*
> *Minutes after they took I*
> *From the bottomless pit*
> *But my heart was made strong*
> *By the hand of the Almighty*
> *We look forward in this generation*
> *Triumphantly*
> *Won't you help me sing*
> *These songs of freedom*
> *For all I ever have*
> *Redemption Songs*

1 MOVEMENT 1

IN THE BEGINNING

US women of the diaspora,
What a genesis,
Are losing life's race to the finish.
Weighted down by the many cloaks of injustice
We are unable to hurdle the fences of malice.

Lighten up, lift up, shed your cover.
Come glide to the beyond and over!

IMAGINE

It is a dark and dreary night as you begin your journey. There are no heavenly stars smiling warmly. Thunderous hisses and lightning kisses are your only guide.

You seek shelter in an abandoned barn. The storm is steadily worsening and bellowing messages of possible harm.

You lie down in an empty, stone-cold manger; it is as unyielding as Eve's unpardonable sentence. You feel so weary and oh so very forlorn.

You drift into restless loneliness, haunted by unpleasant dreams of emptiness. You hear wails coming from beside your head as you lie upon your pillow. Behold, a veiled woman is crouched at your bed. Her wretched form seems so familiar, you are compelled to get to know her.

Her age? The color of her skin? What is she wearing? How long is her hair? Are there shoes on her feet?

You listen to her psalms of the downtrodden. You arise and kneel beside her. She turns her head. She is embarrassed that you will see that her soul is dead. Her eyes are closed, frozen in fright. She cannot see that she is standing in the shadow of her light.

MEET YOUR SLAVE LADY

Hush her tales and hold her hand.
Take her with you to the promised land.
Whisper softly in her ear:
Come journey with me,
Inward to your sleeping soul
And outward to your universe.

LET'S REASON

"In the Beginning" brings us face-to-face with the pain in our lives that we avoid and deny, but must confront and unmask. Begin your journey wherever you feel you are experiencing the most conflict at the moment. For many of us this appears as interpersonal conflicts with family, friends, or peers. For others the conflict is institutionalized, in the form of race and gender inequities. For a few it is spiritual, a yearning for enrichment and a deeper meaning to life. Ultimately, it really does not matter where you start, because the issues are all interwoven and they all have to be dealt with.

My own journey began in the interpersonal realm. After the birth of my first daughter, I felt overwhelmed, trying to balance motherhood, marriage, and career. I was fortunate to engage the services of an outstanding African American female psychiatrist who served as both mentor and role model for me. By understanding how my feelings then were related to unconscious conflicts that arose during my childhood, therapy helped me regain a healthier self-image. The resolution of these conflicts strengthened my sense of worth and the uniqueness of who I am. I became less dependent on others for validation and approval, and relearned how to take charge of my feelings and thoughts. With this "strengthened ego" I began feeling less and less a victim. I was back "in the driver's seat," back in control of my life. Having regained control, I found it much easier to allow myself to be vulnerable, to let go of the need to *always* be in control.

Then came the realization that not only did I want to be less conflicted about here-and-now issues, but I also wanted to find real joy and contentment. This journey has taken me to countless retreats, seminars, workshops, and books on ancient African, Native American, Buddhist, and Hindu religion and science, and brought me to an intimate circle of wonderful women, black and white, all struggling together to find inner peace. This quest for spirit has taught me that experiencing life solely as an individual entity creates boundaries. Ego must be broken through so that the true self can be restored to universal oneness. True inner peace comes with identification as one with creation, one with the supreme life-force. But first, ego must be strengthened, because only a strong ego is able to withstand and survive its dismantling.

For us women of the diaspora, a "strong ego," that is, a healthy self-image that validates our worth, requires more than just working through unconscious conflicts related to family relationships; it requires working through the issues of race and gender inequity, of the wishful fantasy of the "weakened ego" that the perpetrators of oppression will change their evil ways. It requires abolishing the slave mentality of learned helplessness and victimization. Self-reliance, a posture of the "strengthened ego," is expressed in the teachings of the late Bob Marley: "Emancipate yourself from mental slavery, none but ourselves can free our minds." Phrased somewhat differently by Bylle Avery of the National Black Women's Health Project, "We are who we have been waiting for."

The late Malcolm X said that at some point we all must take a trip back to Africa to rid our minds of the negative images of our motherland that we have been fed. That trip can be physical or through books. The cultural self-esteem necessary for my ego-building was strengthened by the writings of Afrocentric Egyptologists and historians such as Yosef A. A. ben-Jochannan, Cheikh Anta Diop, Ivan Van Sertima, Na'im Akbar, Asa Hilliard, Charles Copher, Charles Finch, and Richard King.

In 1990, Billie Jean and I took the physical trip. We journeyed to Zimbabwe with a group of inner-city African American teenagers. There are no words that can adequately describe the intensity of the healing that occurred for all of us, young people and adults alike, during this trip. I was liberated from the images portrayed of our ancestors by Tarzan movies! When I traveled down the mighty Zambezi River, I was able to understand and appreciate how the freedom fighters' superior knowledge of navigating this river led to the death of colonialism in Rhodesia and the birth of Zimbabwe.

I was able to rid myself of the not-good-enough, "welfare mother" image so often projected onto us when I saw African women with their children tied to their backs. I understood then the deep love that we have always had for our children. I felt hopeful that if we could recapture this intense physical and spiritual bonding that we once had with our children, we could win them back and save our families. As one African woman said to me, "How can you put your children in strollers and push them away from you? We like them on our backs. We have few struggles with potty training. We know when they are going to have a movement because we feel them straining upon our backs." Common sense and psychology teach us that children with adequate early-childhood nurturing grow up with self-worth and positive values. I never heard a baby cry in Africa.

In addition to reclaiming the worth of the continent from which we come, we also have to come to terms with the Middle Passage. We must not forget, however, that Africans were in North America prior to slavery; not only were we not slaves then, but we were major contributors to those civilizations. We also must not forget that thousands of slaves escaped or liberated themselves from slavery as maroons or by choosing death.

A deeper understanding of the slave/master dyad also helps to rid us of internalized feelings of inferiority. Supremacists maintain this dyad so that they can experience power. "Massa" defends against his inadequacies and deficiencies by projecting them onto us. (See Dr. Frances Cress Welsing's theory of color confrontation and racism as described in her book, *The Isis Papers*.) To release ourselves from this slave/master dyad, we must reclaim our own self-worth and refuse to accept and act out the projections anymore. We must stop validating Massa's false sense of power by giving ours up. We must, however, continue to operate from love, no matter how enraged we become at the injustices dealt out to us. When one wants to illuminate a

dark room, one adds light, not more darkness. Our empowerment will help return Massa to the true and infinite source within his soul, and remove his need to dominate us.

The Self-Discovery Exercises that follow begin your journey of introspection. Unlike the imaginal discourse, which dealt more with the abstract scars we all have from the wounds of oppression, the daily exercises focus you on your personal history. The abstraction of the discourses only gives the sociocultural contextual framework, the web within which most of our lives operate. The exercises help us get to the core within the external reactions to racism that would keep us in a cycle of helplessness and hopelessness. They begin our process of realizing our true infinite power and potential.

I conduct a support group of African American women living in a housing development. In the beginning, violence, an urgent issue that barrages them daily, was the focus of the group. As the women began to acknowledge the deep pain of their personal losses of the men in their lives—fathers, sons, spouses, brothers, and uncles—a shift occurred. Instead of hoping that some outside agency would begin another anti-violence program in their community, the group mobilized to stop the violence themselves. Their experience of the power within them increased and the pain was released. This made it easier for them to begin to face the deeper personal pains of childhood abuse and neglect.

The Self-Discovery Exercises take you to the relationships in which you experience and play out your life, beginning with your early childhood. Many of us are very reluctant to explore the past. "Let sleeping dogs lie" is our attitude. Is it not better to awaken them gently than to have them come growling ferociously awake? The fact is, the dogs aren't sleeping. They appear dormant because our fragile egos have locked them away behind soundproof doors. They are very much awake and barking inside our unconscious. We sometimes hear them when we sleep, in our dreams, when the ego's doors are open.

We explore our past, not to blame others or ourselves, but instead to understand how past experiences have shaped who we are today. We cannot go back and change painful events; we can only accept that they occurred. By increasing your understanding of how those events affected your thinking, feeling, and behaving patterns, it is easier to develop alternative modes of being. No matter how well-meaning your caretakers were, they could not always adequately meet your needs. This created anxiety that you learned to defend against with varying degrees of avoidance and denial. Such coping skills were necessary so that your body and psyche would not become overwhelmed. But such coping distorted the reality of the experience.

By understanding the circumstances under which our defenses were formed, we can restore our true reality. It also makes it easier to choose to discontinue using these defenses. As adults, we need to face up to our reality and not let childhood patterns continue to dominate our lives. Otherwise we continue the cycle of confusion that eventually leads to dysfunction and despair.

I once worked with a client who became extremely depressed and suicidal every time a relationship ended. In therapy she recalled that when she was about five years old, her mother would leave her alone at nights. Her screaming and pleas did not stop her mother from going. After her mother left, she would lie in bed alone, terrified, eventually crying herself to sleep. She came to realize that as an adult, each time a partner left, she reexperienced the fear of being left alone, just as she had as a child. She realized that this was the source of her current feelings of hopelessness and despair, of wanting to die. She came to understand that it was not her fault that her mother left her at nights to do drugs and prostitute herself. Nothing she could have done or tried to do could have changed the choices that her mother made. She realized that as an adult she was now in control. She also realized that she was no longer helpless or dependent upon her mother, and that by holding on to her fears she was still allowing her mother to control her. She realized that it was now her responsibility to let go of those feelings of abandonment.

SELF-DISCOVERY EXERCISES

Please use your journal for your entries. Take as much writing space and time as you need.

1.

My name is . . .

My age . . .

I was born in . . .

My earliest years were spent in . . .

My earliest memories of my mother are . . .

My earliest memories of my father are . . .

My most memorable teacher was . . .

My teenage years were . . .

My early adult years were (be sure to include family and romantic relationships, in addition to career) . . .

I first became aware of racism when . . .

Since then, racism has affected my life in the following way(s): . . .

My late adult years have been (be sure to include family and romantic relationships, in addition to career) . . .

The most significant event in my life thus far has been . . .

The symbol that best describes me right now is (for example, "I feel like a butterfly emerging from her cocoon") . . .

2.

The last time I felt sad was . . .

I told myself the following about

a. myself . . .

b. the other person(s) involved (if any) . . .

3.

The last time I felt mad was . . .

I told myself the following about

a. myself . . .

b. the other person(s) involved (if any) . . .

4.

The theme common to both those situations in which I felt sad and mad is . . .

Some other instances in which I have had similar responses are . . .

5.

What I fear the most is . . .

Some of my other fears are . . .

6.

I think I am losing control when . . .

The part of my body in which I most experience that feeling of powerlessness is . . .

RELEASING EXERCISE NO. 1

This is an experience of the mask of denial, our coverup.

Create or purchase a mask; put it on and become aware of your feelings behind the mask. Who is hiding? From whom? From what? Is there a pattern? Can you let the real person behind the mask emerge?

Doing this exercise makes me

a. feel . . .

b. think . . .

Your pain is the breaking of the shell that encloses your pain.
—Kahlil Gibran

2 MOVEMENT 2
DAWN

US women of the diaspora
Yes, cry foul!
Anesthetize our slumbering souls
In the dungeons of the living dead.
We cannot feel the joy waiting ahead.

Arise from your numbing plight!
Open up to the goddess of light!

I MAGINE

It is long past midnight, close to morning. Dawn is preparing to be reborn. Gently she kisses your sleeping head, awakening you.

She invites you to join her mystery function, held daily in her court at the Rainbow junction. Gladly you escape sleep's hard, cold bosom and you waltz through her garden of morning glory, red roses, orange mums, yellow daisies, green ferns, blue lilies, purple freesias, white gardenias.

You inhale the fragrant blooms and sip the pure morning dew. You groove to the flutes of the angels. Your cup surely runneth over with music.

You suspend all thoughts and place them next to your heart. You delve into the still darkness, drifting, drifting, feeling light as a lark.

Deeper and deeper you sink into reverie, into the

rhapsody of time immortal. A trumpet sounds. Your timeless spell is broken. The music goes dead.

In the dark skies, chariots burst forth upon the horizon, drawn by cherubs swathed in glittering red. Velvet curtains begin to open. Slowly, silently, the sun lifts her golden head. Triumphantly she strides, spraying kisses from red-painted lips. You chant her wondrous praise, as you linger in her majestic grip. You scream out loud to the virgin sky, I TOO HAVE COME ALIVE!

LET'S REASON

"Dawn" depicts our reconnection to the simple beauty that surrounds us in nature. It is the complement to the first movement, the joyous calm that comes after the storm. It reminds us that if we take off the blinders of our pain, we will see too that we have much joy.

"In the Beginning" and "Dawn" symbolize the acceptance of both the negative and positive forces in our lives. Without one, the other does not exist. One of the major principles of Gestalt theory is that we become aware of an object in relationship to its contrasting background. For example, we cannot perceive light except in contrast to darkness, motion except in contrast to rest, pleasure except in contrast to pain.

When our psyches become wounded, we bury and wall off the pain from the rest of the body. With time, this wall becomes thicker and thicker, until eventually an impermeable scar is formed, letting nothing in or out. As we block pain, so too we block pleasure. This is very similar to the formation of an abscess, in which the body forms a wall to block the pus from escaping and doing more harm. In so doing, the entry of the cells of the immune system to battle the infecting organisms is also blocked. If the abscess is left untreated, it will eventually burst and infect the rest of the body. In most instances, however, if the abcess is lanced and drained, the body quickly heals. We are often afraid of the lancing because we fear the pain.

If we tolerate the transient pain, the release of the pus brings permanent relief. The same is true with psychic wounds. If we allow ourselves to tolerate the transient pain of breaking down our defenses, the hurt will come pouring out, followed by joy.

The underlying trigger for our feelings of hurt, sadness, and anger is fear, the perception of threat to our survival. Fear creates disharmony and imbalance—and hence stress—in our bodies because it triggers the "fight-or-flight" response of the autonomic nervous system. This is an evolutionary system in which our bodily functions optimize our ability to fight or escape. In his book *Ageless Body, Timeless Mind,* Deepak Chopra describes three phases to the stress response: the event, the appraisal, the body's reaction. He argues that the appraisal phase is the vital link, the bridge between the event and the response. Appraisal is under our control and is influenced by our memories of similar past experiences. The degree to which the event triggers memories of potential threat is the extent to which the autonomic nervous system will be activated. Chronic fear resulting from unresolved or unreleased hurt and/or anger disrupts the normal metabolic processes and produces stress-related disorders. Dr. Chopra cites the following experiment with rats in which they lose their freedom: "When rats are crowded together like tenants in a tenement project, their immune systems decline and show signs of hypertension, neurosis, apathy, and depression." Does it come as a surprise that hypertension and diabetes, two illnesses linked to excessive stress, are among the major killers of African American women?

I was awestruck the first time I visited Mosi Oi Tunya (called Victoria Falls by the colonialists), during my trip to Zimbabwe. I was amazed by the incredible beauty of the Zambezi River bellowing mist high into the skies as it thunderously roared to its fall. So in awe was I that I made a return trip, during which I made the following entry in my diary:

> Unlike the first trip with Billie Jean and the group, there was no rainbow awaiting me today when I arrived at the falls. It was dark and overcast. Perhaps I should have gone with the rest of the group on the trip to the marketplace. On my solitary walk along the treacherous paths, I was alone and afraid. At times I could barely see while walking because the water sprays were so powerful. But for some unknown reason I decided to continue to the end. Gradually I stopped fighting the water. Then with each spray I began feel-

ing more cleansed, as if my sins were being washed away. By the end of the trail I felt light and free, renewed. A feeling of serenity and creativity was unleashed within me. When I returned to the mouth of the falls, guess what was waiting to greet me? Not only was there the most spectacular rainbow I had ever seen, it was a double! And to think I would have missed it if I had turned back.

I had a similar experience during a trip Billie Jean and I made to Frankfurt, Germany. Every morning we went to the spa to work out. The first morning, after a steaming hot sauna, Billie Jean plunged into the ice-cold bath. Euphoric from her experience, she invited me to follow, but I declined. I did not think I could physically endure the rapid temperature change; my body would go into shock. The second day my competitive nature compelled me to respond to the challenge. Shivering even before I put my foot in, I braced and told myself to let go and jump in, full body. As I plunged into the water, the most incredible sensation of pleasure overcame me. I felt tingles all over. I could not wait to get back in the next day.

I have noticed how much more pleasurable therapy is for my clients after they break through their fear and appreciate the privilege of spending time with themselves. One client, a young African American pro-fessional woman, sought therapy because of worsening feelings of depression. She felt blue most of the time, like a zombie going through the motions of her daily routine. Exploration revealed that when she was an adolescent, she had taken on the task of nurturing her father and siblings after her mother's death. In doing so, she avoided her intense anger at her mother for not having been honest about how sick she was. Stepping into the role of mother also helped her avoid the deep sadness of losing her mother; her mother lived on through her. During therapy, some twenty years later, she slowly began grieving, letting go of the sadness and anger. In so doing, she was able to shed the bur-den of being the "idealized" mother, and began grow-ing and blossoming into her own self.

One of the major issues she had to confront was her pattern of choosing relationships with emotionally abusive men. She realized she was emulat-ing her mother, who had allowed her father to control her totally. She also realized that she became paralyzed in these relationships in fear of being left, as her mother had left her. She was afraid that being assertive would make the men go away. As she began to work on these dysfunctional behaviors, her mother appeared to her in a dream for the first time since her death. At first she was afraid. When she eventually looked up, her mother was looking into her eyes and smiling with her. She cried for a while. Upon awakening the next morning, she felt joyful. Seeing her mother's smiling face allowed her to let go of the painful image she had carried for all these years of her lying motionless, still and leathery, in her coffin. Soon thereafter she began spending more healing time with herself in activities that led her closer to self-discovery. She made a career change to a more ful-filling job. She began dating someone with whom she felt free to be herself. Her eyes, too, are smiling now. Her spirit has reawakened.

The Self-Discovery Exercises are meant to increase your awareness of the pleasure zones that naturally surround you—the people, places, and things that bring you happiness. By reminding yourself that there is much goodness all around you in your daily life, you will make yourself better able to weather your inevitable storms.

SELF-DISCOVERY EXERCISES

7.

My favorite time of day is (explain) . . .

My favorite flower is (explain) . . .

My favorite animal is (explain) . . .

My favorite holiday is (explain) . . .

My favorite person is . . .

8.

The best period of my life was . . .

9.

The last time I felt joy was . . .

I told myself the following about

a. myself . . .

b. the other person(s) (if any) . . .

10.

The last time I felt at peace was . . .

I told myself the following about

a. myself . . .

b. the other person(s) (if any) . . .

11.

The theme common to both of those situations in which I felt joy and peace is . . .

Other situations in which I have had these same feelings are . . .

12.

The last time I thought I was in control of my emotions was . . .

Other situations in which I have had similar thoughts of being in control are . . .

RELEASING EXERCISE NO. 2

This gives you an experience of the power of awakening into the light, from the dark of night.

Wake up one morning before sunrise. If you can face the east and watch the sunrise, do so. If not, just observe the morning become light around you. As you watch in solitude, recall a time in your early life when you felt free of inhibitions, full of dreams and ideals. What were your aspirations then? Where are they now? Record your thoughts in your journal.

Doing this exercise makes me

a. feel . . .

b. think . . .

Together with the exercises in "In the Beginning," these cleansing steps are intended to harmonize and unify your experience of the opposites in your life; they are not meant to eradicate or deny their existence. The aim is to help you take the pain with the pleasure, the pleasure with the pain.

"Three Little Birds," a song by Bob Marley, reminds us of this joy:

Don't worry about a thing
'Cause every little thing is going to be all right.
Woke up this morning, smiled with the rising sun
Three little birds beside my doorstep
Singing sweet songs of melodies pure and true
Singing, This is my message to you
Singing, Don't worry about a thing
'Cause every little thing is going to be all right.

Your joy is your sorrow unmasked.
—Kahlil Gibran

MOVEMENT 3

THE VALLEY OF THE SHADOW OF LIFE

US women of the diaspora
We do feel beat!
Always cover up our bunioned feet,
Trying to escape the bumps we meet.
"No more bruises, please," we plead.

Kick off those burning shoes! Get those feet nude!
Come reign fresh on your parade with new attitude!

IMAGINE

It is early morning; you leave Eden. Continue you must the search for deliverance. Good-bye to self-pity and wretched penance!

A bevy of merrily buzzing bees beckons you to flit through the pregnant valley, bursting red with flowers.

Rose-colored butterflies, frolicking, pluck red rose petals and throw them at your feet. "Queen for a day," the royal carpet greets you.

"Your highness," a nearby stream gurgles the invitation, "let me rub those tired feet with my rocks, as smooth as polished beads. Next, my red-bellied fish-in-waiting, all eager and ready, will strum tunes on those soles, bound to make you tingle."

You succumb to queenly leisure, exploding as you surrender to pleasure. Totally exhausted from your trembling, you seek sanctuary in your soul. It never shivers!

You notice some red-bellied birds hovering high above, whistling you to come rest in their forest, their secret haven away from mother sky.

You lie beneath a poinciana tree, its blossoms flaming crimson like the Red Sea, the giant roots as your anchor, the fallen leaves your cover. Your awareness begins to extend outward to the branches' end.

You breathe deeply and slowly, inhaling nature's calm and exhaling your worry. With the divine exchange of energy, you loosen the hold of your tight muscles; slowly they give up their relentless fighting.

You sink deep into your floating body, spirit soaring as your soul ascends. You find the space between the breaths, where nothing exists but the eternal self. All boundaries disappear. Into the belly of the earth you fall. Swallowed up, You become one with All!

LET'S REASON

"The Valley of the Shadow of Life" depicts a process of reconnecting to nature, to become revitalized and grounded in its infinite power. This imaginal discourse corresponds to the first chakra, the root chakra. This chakra receives the energy bubbling up from the center of the earth; it is one of high physical energy and strength. It is represented in the spectrum by red, the color of warm fire, and blood, the physical juice of life.

African-descended people were once deeply rooted in the earth and all her rhythms. Western culture is currently one of conquest and domination of nature. We seem to have adopted this once-alien principle.

Perhaps our forced labor upon her soil during slavery made us angry with her. Maybe we blamed her for our plight, like the slaves in Jamaica after emancipation, who wanted nothing to do with the land and refused the little they were allotted. How long can we afford to stay angry at her? Our collective unconscious knows of her purity and the fury of her power unleashed. Where is our leadership in the environmental movement?

The more disconnected we have become from nature and her power, the more we see power as material and external, and not part of our internal connection to the earth. By internalizing the power of nature, we feel our own power and become much less competitive and dependent in our interpersonal relationships.

In my early childhood, growing up in Jamaica, I was very connected to the earth. I was the youngest, and my siblings were very much older. Even though I was alone a lot, I never felt lonely. On visits to my parents' home in the country, I would spend most of my time outdoors. I was free to roam; I could pick whatever fruits I wanted, go to any river, play on anyone's land. Looking back now, I see that the village belonged to me, and I to it. What power! There was a meadow by the house where I would play for hours. One of my favorite pastimes was to lie under a huge poinciana tree, imagining myself all grown up. I would create stories in my head of what my life would be when I grew up. In all these mini–soap operas, I portrayed myself in grandeur. My sense of self knew no limits. This all changed during high school, when I went to a boarding school where I lived with the rich colonialists. For the first time in my life I felt poor and inferior. My self-esteem was severely damaged. I was robbed of my power, although now I understand that I participated in giving it up. I managed to succeed intellectually, but at a high price.

The pain of this injured self resurfaced in the beginning years of my marriage. I had expectations that my husband was responsible for making me feel worthy and good about myself. I transferred onto him my unmet needs to feel whole: *Love me so that I know I am lovable!* As I began to grow spiritually, I reopened my eyes to the source of real power, my connection to the infinite power in nature, that I had experienced in my early childhood. I gradually lessened my dependence on him, and our relationship significantly improved. My needs are now my responsibility to fulfill. If he chooses to complement my fulfillment of those needs, great, but I no longer see it as his responsibility. I don't need him to love me in order to feel lovable. I feel good about myself once again because I know that I am a part of this wondrous garden of life; I feel beautiful because I know that the flowers, the sunset, the waterfalls, the trees, the birds and butterflies are a part of me; I mirror their beauty in me.

My connection to the universal power source was greatly reinforced during my visit to the waterfalls at Mosi Oi Tunya. As I walked along the path and became overpowered by the water sprays drenching me, I inhaled and brought its force into me. With each exhalation I shed a piece of my insecurity—I was not pretty enough, smart enough, good enough. I felt its electricity flow through me, and left with a very strong connection to that power.

Every African American woman I have seen in therapy has been afflicted with some level of this codependency. I can always gauge when my clients are feeling better by the degree to which their feeling good about themselves is not relationship-based. I thoroughly enjoyed Terry McMillan's book *Waiting to Exhale,* but it left me feeling very sad. She so eloquently captured a sad truth of us African-descended women; the breathing that fuels our life too often depends on someone else!

The Self-Discovery Exercises that follow begin with your family. They are meant to have you explore the nature of your connectedness. You chose this earth family because they have important lessons to teach you, and you them. The exercises then branch out to the friends and groups of people whom you more consciously selected. Do you drain relationships to fulfill your ego needs? Try to figure out the purpose of these people in your life, whether they help you get closer to your mission in life, or farther away from it.

SELF-DISCOVERY EXERCISES

13.

This is my family tree (add in as many members as possible) . . .

14.

I am most similar to the following person(s) in my family (explain) . . .

15.

I am most different from the following person(s) in my family (explain) . . .

16.

The person(s) in my family to whom I turn for support is (explain) . . .

The friend to whom I turn to for support is (explain) . . .

Overall, the person whom I feel the most supported by is (explain) . . .

17.

I belong to the following community/state organizations (or am involved in the following activities) . . .

I belong to the following national organizations (or am involved in the following activities) . . .

I belong to the following international organizations (or am involved in the following activities) . . .

RELEASING EXERCISE NO. 3

This is an experience of your own relatedness to nature.

Take a trip (close by if at all possible) to your favorite place outdoors—mountains, ocean, lake, river, desert, or simply a park if you are city-bound. Free yourself of all distractions. Spend at least four hours by yourself observing nature. Write an essay describing your experience. You could title it, for example, "My Personal Space in Nature."

Doing this exercise makes me

a. feel . . .

b. think . . .

The intent of this exercise is to help you build a stronger bond with nature so that you can become less emotionally dependent upon and possessive of your people-tree, so that you might relate to the people as they are, not as the people you would like them to be.

And forget not that the earth delights to feel your bare feet and the wind longs to play with your hair.
—Kahlil Gibran

MOVEMENT 4

4 FIRE DANCE

US women of the diaspora
Oh so very fine
No longer honor our bodies divine.
Dodging assault and battery of every kind
We turn off our sacred grind.

Slip back into your rhythmic all!
Come rock-steady at the fireball!

IMAGINE

It is high noon. You leave the royal forest, headed for the golden foothills, searching for wilderness. The sun is fierce. Amid her centered radiance she erases your shadow, spinning you into trance. Spellbound, you begin a motionless dance.

You sit in the hollow by the lake. A mermaid emerges and beckons you to enter. You dive into her outstretched arms, lazily swimming through her aqua bed. When your scorching soul is quenched and you are replenished, you arise from her erotic hold.

Eager to show your dance, you prance though orange meadows blazing with ripened sunflowers. You join the sun-drenched crickets preparing for midday bacchanal. "Creatures of pleasure," is their call:

> *Their drum beats*
> *Your heart leaps*
> *Faster and faster*
> *Louder and louder*
> *Hotter and hotter*
> *Wilder and wilder . . .*

You sip the sweet, warm nectar freshly prepared by the queen bee. You savor the liquid jubilee!

The darting neon fireflies charge the air with desire. Your soul, once ice, is now on fire.

You whirl in bliss,
 All aglow with ecstasy.
  You become the music, the dance electric:
   Your head and your shoulders,
    Your arms and your feet.

You pulsate in stillness to the silent music.
 Surely, purely orgasmic.
  You reclaim your creativity!

L ET'S REASON

"Fire Dance" recognizes and celebrates the rhythm, beauty, and generativity of our physical self. It is an experience in knowing and loving our bodies! This movement corresponds to the second chakra, the splenic chakra. It is the center of our creative energies, especially those of the genital procreative areas. The color is orange, the warm, intimate color of blazing sun and fire.

Often for us women of the diaspora, the news of pregnancy or a sexually transmitted disease comes as a surprise. Where were we when it was happening? Why weren't we fully there? Why do we so often fail to be fully, mentally, present for sex?

This surely is not a derivative of our ancestral past. During our visit to Zimbabwe, I attended an initiation ceremony in a rural village. "We are a people of love," said the Mkishi dancer. "All our lives we are taught about love." He rocked his pelvis—*bim, bim, bam*—as he demonstrated the dance of initiated boys trying to get chosen by the chief's daughter. "Sex is technical," he went on. "Our elders teach us how."

In my practice, at least fifty percent of the African-descended women have been molested. Too many women of the diaspora can testify to unconsenting sex, ranging from violent rape by a stranger to the date that ended in rape. Unlike white women clients, women of the diaspora appear much less angry with their recollections of these events, getting angry with *me* sometimes for using the word *violation* or for refusing to collude with them in thinking that what happened to them was okay: "No, an eleven-year-old cannot freely give consent—even if it is with Daddy or Reverend so-and-so!" It seems that we have come to accept this as a normal and routine part of our course.

During slavery, our bodies were used and abused, raped for Massa's pleasure and pocket. Now our men often treat us as Massa once did. Torn apart from our elders, with no one to teach us healthy sexual attitudes, perhaps our men learned such abuse from Massa. And we have not learned that part of our freedom from chattel slavery is our right to say no in reference to our bodies.

A thirtyish African American professional woman client reported a recurrent dream of hearing footsteps coming into her room, beginning at about age four. When she told her mother about it, her mother responded that she was having bad dreams because she did not say her prayers. Years later, she was raped in college. She did not tell her mother; instead she slit her wrists. During her therapy she was engaged in a sexually abusive relationship in which she often disassociated during sex. She simply was not there; she didn't allow herself to feel.

We must truly value our bodies. This means consenting mentally and physically every time it is being entered. We get very angry when someone breaks into our house or car! Yet we have become disconnected from the outrage we justifiably experience when our bodies are violated.

The constant denigration of our Negroid physical features, too, leaves us feeling violated and degraded. We are not the ones portrayed as beautiful and desirable, to be adored and "made love" to. We have internalized the portrayals of our "ugliness," the result being that many of us despise our bodies. We accept the role of "fuck objects." If *we* do not love our bodies, how can we expect physical loving from someone else?

A client wept inconsolably as she recalled being laughed at and called Aunt Jemima by her friends at age six. She grew up feeling so ugly, she would quickly consent to anyone who wanted her body. The scars haunted her even while she embarked upon a prestigious professional career. None of the men she has dated have mirrored her accomplishments.

Are you, too, a professional woman who thinks she is ugly and will never find a partner? I've observed in my practice that clients who feel this way often immerse themselves totally in their work and do not give themselves opportunities to meet and make partnerships. They do so to avoid the fear that they will be rejected, not chosen. By so limiting the chances of meeting a mate, they invariably have greater difficulties. This creates a self-fulfilling prophecy; it reinforces their feelings that they are not attractive and desirable, and makes them isolate themselves even more. Black women doctors and attorneys seem to be pros at this. There is certainly some validity in these feelings of undesirability, for many of these women have watched a majority of their male professional counterparts choose European-featured partners.

A client of mine, a brilliant Negroid-featured attorney, became so accustomed to a lack of interest from her black male professional peers that she always took on the role of organizer ("professional mammy") within the dominantly male local society organization. She never saw this as a potential source for a partner, even in her desperation to find one. The deeper issue for this woman, was the haunting memory of growing up as an "ugly sister." Her paler-skinned sister with "good hair" was the one who always had the dates; it was this sister who always got asked to dance at the parties while she sat watching; it was this sister who always got chosen for the part of leading lady in the school plays. All her life, my client felt devoid of beauty. Carrying this feeling over into adulthood, she never expected to be chosen by the men to whom she was attracted—other successful professional men. In fact, with these men she projected a lack of interest in dating them, to cover her deep fears of being rejected by them. Instead she chose men with whom she felt she couldn't lose—those of lesser means who were attracted to her money.

Do you date "no-good hustling" men who rip you off and take your money, because you feel that you cannot do better? At a recent meeting of black women physicians, it was striking to note how many were married to financial planners. Whose estates are they planning, whose money are they investing? I have seen many black women settle for nonprofessional spouses. Their attitude is that it is better to have less than none at all. This is certainly not their professional demeanor; they are always aspiring to do better. For many, tremendous conflicts eventually arise around issues of control.

Do you overlook clues to bisexuality in a man? In the United States, African Americans are the group with the highest rate of HIV infection. One of the significant contributors to the rapid spread of HIV in the African American community is the denial of bisexuality among our men. I have worked with several HIV-positive African American men who contracted the disease through sex with other men, but have refused to label those encounters as homosexual.

Do you marginalize your lesbian sisters, afraid it is contagious? Could it be that your resistance has been lowered by the repressed rage you feel at men, the many times you literally wanted to "fuck him to death"? Could it be that you fear that if a lesbian sister gets too close, you just might go "that other way"? Perhaps we can lessen our fear of homosexual contamination by healing our heterosexual relationships. Do you avoid emotional intimacy with your sisters for fear you could be labeled "gay" (a more subtle form of homophobia)? Could it be that we are afraid to be close to our sisters because of latent fears of homosexuality? Would we rather not have any stimuli that could awaken those dormant desires?

Do you think of masturbation as dirty? Are you afraid or unable to satisfy your need for sexual release?

A client of mine was only able to talk about her frequent masturbation when she became panicked that she might be damaging her vulva. She was ashamed because she wanted to be perceived as a good religious woman. Even though she felt like a "bad" person, she could not stop because it was her only source of sexual pleasure. Sex with her partner was unfulfilling and she engaged in it with him only for his pleasure. We pondered together whether a loving God would get angry with her for finding pleasure in the body that He (her pronoun) gave her to enjoy. Her shame diminished significantly. In addition to shame, many African-descended women have disconnected from the pleasure of touch out of fear. For so many, their earlier experiences have been negative—excessive corporal punishment and/or inappropriate sexual touching. To avoid the pain and shame, we no longer touch ourselves or ask to be touched. Once again, we give up the pleasure in avoidance of the pain.

Healthy sexuality is the attitude of acknowledging and enjoying bodily pleasure. It begins with a strong and healthy ego, one that values and respects the body. A strengthened ego is a stepping-stone to revering our bodies as a sacred space. Healthy sexuality requires engaging in body care that helps to reawaken the pleasure of touch and sound vibrations, and becoming familiar with our pleasure zones. Such care requires that we keep our bodies clean, relaxed, moisturized, and well toned. With body and mind in harmony, sexual union becomes a celebration of spirit—a waltz between spirits enlarging, transcending their boundaries, and collapsing into one—the "Fire Dance."

Given the alarming increase in sexually transmitted diseases and unintended pregnancies, especially among our youth, we African-descended women can no longer afford not to place an extremely high value on our bodies. Unfortunately, many of us do not assert our worth because we are afraid of losing our relationships. Our culture is one in which "being in a relationship" is a key determinant of self-worth. A client once remarked that "a bad man is better than no man." "I'm happiest when I have a man" is another attitude I frequently hear. Could it be that for us women of the diaspora, self-nothingness, the death instinct, is driven by relationship loss?

The following Self-Discovery Exercises encourage you to explore your feelings about your body and your sexuality. Be very honest; how you feel about your physical self becomes projected onto how you feel about your total self. It influences the way you interact in relationships with family, mates, and professional colleagues.

SELF-DISCOVERY EXERCISES

18.

I think that my hair is . . .

I think that my lips are . . .

I think that my nose is . . .

I think that my hips are . . .

I think that my feet are . . .

I think that my skin color is . . .

19.

The part of my body that I am the most ashamed of is (explain) . . .

The part of my body that I most like to show off is (explain) . . .

20.

I experience and define my sexuality . . .

Enjoyable sex for me means . . .

RELEASING EXERCISE NO. 4

This is an experience in feeling your body in all its auto-erotic zones.

Take a relaxing bath in sea salts. Have candles lit, incense burning, and soft music playing. While your body is still wet, massage yourself all over with bath oil. Emerge from your bath and dance naked in front of a full-length mirror. Feel the rhythm of your body as it moves. Say something affirming about each part of your body—in particular your hair, lips, hips, skin tone, and feet. (For example, for dark-hued sisters, "I honor the richness of my dark skin." For light-hued sisters, "I honor the radiance of my tan skin.")

Doing this exercise makes me:

a. feel . . .

b. think . . .

And your body is the harp of your soul,
And it brings forth sweet music from
it or confused sounds.
—Kahlil Gibran

This poem is a tribute to all our unfortunate brothers
and sisters whose quest for love ended in death. Thank
you for teaching us to be more safe!

TO WALKER

Hush, dear Walker,
Let me wipe the last remaining
    tear
So that you might fly tall
Triumphantly into Spirit Hall
Without sadness or fear.

Let me guide you
To your mother's side,
So that you might reawaken
her gleaming pride
and bring back the memories of
    joy
Of having been the vessel for you
Her first darling boy.

Move next to your father
Show him the start
of releasing the sorrow
That grips his grieving heart.

Join both their hands
Whisper softly in their ears:
Thank you for the many wondrous
    years.
Blow gently upon their eyes,
    swollen with pain
Tell them that loving you was not
    in vain.

Sweet journeys of peace to your vi-
brant, beating soul
Till we meet once more in our in
visible temple of gold.

5 MOVEMENT 5

THE HEALING WATERS

US women of the diaspora
Yes, we need teddy bears!
All have stories to tell
Of our invisible fears
Secretly locked away,
All these many years.
For when we shouted,
No one seemed to hear,
Or care.

Whisper softly into the healing water,
Watch talk change to harmless vapor.

IMAGINE

It is midafternoon; how you wish it would rain. The sun is still so very hot and high.

You journey down the rugged mountain, seeking the ocean. The flowing waters, you've been told, wash away useless ego and pride, leaving one with nothing to hide.

You rest next to a cliff smoking thunder down its waterfall. With the piercing wind trying to color you blue, you blanket beneath the warm sun's yellow hue.

You observe a droplet as it separates from the flow

and rises up, only to fall back to its source, reborn. As you quietly ponder this wonder, the waves, a quiet thunder, rise up and rock you. Back and forth you ride their never-ending course, slowly eroding layer after layer of yourself. Stripped bare, down to the core, your soul is now fully exposed and set free.

You lift off and soar to the one whose hurt has been hardest for you to endure. You bid this one come close, to hear how he or she has caused you so much sadness and fear. You listen as he or she tells of living hell, of feeling like Judas. Recognizing each other's pain, you exchange solemn vows of repentance.

Lighter still in truth, you float to the one whom you have brought the most sorrow. It cannot wait for tomorrow. You listen as he or she tells you how love and trust become sadness and anger. You tell him or her that you're sorry for all the pain and worry.

Together, in loving embrace, you both wash away bitter tears, ones that previously stung so sharply.

You join the droplet. You enter the circular spiral of the flow of life and death. You release all past and present fears, slipping tomorrows into yesterdays.

LET'S REASON

"The Healing Waters" depicts forgiveness and the release of the emotional scars of relationships gone wrong. This movement challenges us to empathize with our weakened spirit as both victim and perpetrator of pain. It continues the cleansing work of the first two movements, but in a more personal way. The Healing Waters corresponds to the third chakra, the solar plexus chakra. It is the center of the emotions, giving balance and clarity to feelings and thought. Its color is warm yellow, that of the sun glowing softly.

In my clinical experience, it has been fascinating to observe that women initially believe they chose relations with men who were like their fathers, only to discover upon deeper exploration that their choices in a mate are much more like their mothers. The focus shifts to the mother, and she consumes the rest of the therapy.

For many African American women, exploring their relationships with their mothers is very difficult. They feel that doing so is being disloyal. It is hard to admit to anger toward one's mother because we feel that we cannot be angry at someone we love. There seems to be a deep-seated fear that our mothers will withdraw their love if they know that we are angry with them. As one of my clients stated, "I can only have Mother's love by being attached to her."

Is it possible that we are still yearning for that earlier time in the motherland when we were physically attached to our mother—tied to her back all day, by her bosom throughout much of the night? Does not having been tied to her make us feel unloved by her now, abandoned? Is that why it is so hard to let go? Do we feel that we never had enough of her touch? How painful it must have been for our slave mothers not to have us tied to them, not to feel our soothing warmth upon their backs as they toiled the long, hard hours, not to know that we were okay because we were with them. Is that why we mothers still won't let our children go?

During my visit to Zimbabwe, I noticed that many Africans seemed unaffected by high levels of anxiety. I was struck by how very much at ease they seemed. Those of us from America were always the ones with reservations and fears. We were the ones who spent our babyhood in strollers. They were the ones with the security of their mothers' backs. (Isn't it interesting that one of our expressions of supporting someone is "I got your back"?) I have also observed the attitudes of African students in classroom settings. They possess a great sense of self and of confidence about their abilities, not worrying much about what others may think. Do children who have had the security of being firmly attached grow up more able to spread their wings?

Us women of the African diaspora must forgive our mothers for not meeting all our needs. We must forgive their shortcomings. But first we have to acknowledge the anger. Our mother will not stop loving us. Deep within, she knows when she has let us down. She is afraid to show us her pain, her vulnerability. She feels that she must be strong so that we will not make the same mistakes she has made. She won't tell us that she faced the same issues we are now facing. She won't talk about sex except to say, "Better not come home with no baby, no belly."

"I will never be like her when I grow up," many of us say. A woman may be angry that her mother didn't leave her abusive man. We won't ever stick with a man as she did for too long trying to work things out. Another woman may be angry because her mother left that abusive man. We yearn for him now. It was her

fault all along. And we hang in there with our man. We know that he will change one day and start treating us well.

A woman may be angry that her mother didn't stop the molestation she received from her man. She gets the brunt of the anger. I have observed that what makes the majority of my clients angry is not the perpetrator's actions so much as the absence of a mother to protect them. So angry are we that we forget that she too was a victim, as was her mother and her mother's mother. So immobilized and silenced have these many generations of black women been by their unspoken pain that their secrets have been all but forgotten. In some way, however small or unintentional, they must

have contributed to your finding the voice to speak out and break the cycle.

A woman may be angry that her mother held her back, that she clipped her wings. She didn't let us take that one chance we had to go off and realize our dreams of success, of fortune and fame. She needed us with her so that we might help her manage the household, care for the other kids. Where is the mate who promised always to be by her side? The rest of the family for whom she is always there? The friends to whom she always lends a helping hand? Could she have been trying to hold on to her last bit of pride, pretending that together you could show the world that you could get by?

By forgiving Mother, we free ourselves to be our own woman. Often that turns out to be just like Mother. By being less angry at Mother, we can be very comforted to hear ourselves sound just like her, speak in that familiar voice. I have been actively involved in women's reproductive health rights throughout my career. I was surprised when I learned that in the 1930s my mother was very involved in birth-control distribution and arranging "losing belly" in Jamaica. She always seemed to have such conservative views in comparison to mine.

We too must ask our mothers' forgiveness for all the demands we make of them to satisfy our needs, often at the expense of their own. As children our mouths were always open, always wanting to be fed. In vain they tried to fill our bottomless pits. Recall all the times that they gave up taking a vacation so that we could go off with our friends instead. Or the times they had to get additional work, already worn out from the regular nine-to-five, so that we could have the most stunning gown for the prom, the TV in our rooms, on and on. We didn't fully understand then what being a mother meant; we did not know that she was not omnipotent.

We must ask Mother's forgiveness for doing the very things from which she tried to protect us. All the times we wanted to find out on our own that the fire was hot, then expected her to nurse our burns without comment. So many of us get angry at our mothers for not being totally supportive of our spousal choices. Then later on we get angry again that they were not supportive during the divorce.

We must ask our children's forgiveness for doing to them the very same things that we were angry at our mothers for doing to us. A client became enraged when she found out that her daughter was living with her fiancé. She refused to attend the wedding, stating that her daughter was dead in her heart. My client's pregnancy out of wedlock with this very daughter had resulted in her own mother's abandonment of her for many years. This news reawakened all her buried turmoil. Because they were insufficiently resolved at the time, she repeated the same painful behaviors with her daughter that were inflicted upon her by her mother—abandonment of loved ones who disappoint us by repeating our mistakes. We must ask our children's forgiveness for expecting them to live our unfulfilled wishes.

We must ask our mates' forgiveness for wanting them to be the ideal parents we never had, and being angry at them when they could not. A client of mine summed up her fourteen-year marriage in the following way: "We have been busy trying to change each other into improved versions of our own mothers."

Equally important, we must forgive ourselves for not being able to meet the unrealistic standards we have set for ourselves, for wanting to please everyone and be liked all the time by children, parents, spouses, siblings, friends, professional peers. Forgiveness of self and others reminds us that we are all just human after all, in all our splendor and disgrace.

The purpose of the Releasing Exercise that follows is to help us let go of anger at others by seeing the same potential in ourselves to inflict pain and hurt upon others. We stay angry at others because we fear their power to hurt us. We lose our power in these situations because we have perceived more power in the other person. By recognizing the same energies in yourself, you defuse your fear, let go of your anger, and take back your power. You forgive.

SELF-DISCOVERY EXERCISES

21.

In my early childhood I was hurt most by . . .

In my teenage years I was hurt most by . . .

In my adult years I have been hurt most by . . .

If only my mother could have protected me from . . .

22.

The person whom I have hurt the most is
(explain) . . .

The person whom I have loved the most is
(explain) . . .

RELEASING EXERCISE NO. 5

Write a letter to the person with whom you are most angry, telling them why. Can you see their negative qualities in yourself? Probably not, since they have been projected onto this enemy. Ask their forgiveness. If you acknowledge these negative qualities in yourself, it will be easy to do so. You may or may not choose to mail this letter.

Doing this exercise makes me:

a. feel . . .

b. think . . .

For love that seeks aught but the disclosure of its own mystery is not love but a net cast forth: and only the unprofitable is caught.
—Kahlil Gibran

6 MOVEMENT 6

THE SEA OF LOVE

US women of the diaspora
Yes, give us glamour!
Keep bobbing for knights
Looking for shining armor.
Wobbling instead
In cauldrons of chaos
We cannot feel the love
That truly surrounds us.

Lie still! Don't bounce!
Slow down your quicksand motion
Come flow in the real love potion!

IMAGINE

It is late afternoon. You descend from the cliffs, seeking siesta. The sea, resting quietly beneath her turquoise sheet, beckons you to come take refuge from the glaring heat.

Longing for the comfort of her mighty womb, you wrap your soul in her soothing arms, ever so tightly. You immerse your head in her lightly beating heart. You lose yourself in the waves of her thick love nectar. Shipwrecked maybe, but ready for adventure.

You awaken upon the shores of a deserted isle.

Time seems to have stopped for a very long while. All the shades of green surround you. Such enchanted beauty as this your eyes have never seen.

Myrtle trees swaying in the breeze whistle tunes that melt your frozen, unrequited loves, hearts that never united. As you roam carefree through the open green fields, all of love's heartaches become unleashed.

You approach an iridescent archway sparkling with emerald ferns. You behold the sacred Goddess, adorned with bright flowers and gems, seated upon her translucent throne.

You fall to your knees and kiss her holy feet. She beckons you come close and share her seat. As you move into her tender embrace, she wipes the endless tears flowing from your face. She feeds you berries from her golden bowl, ending the years of famine starving your soul.

She adorns you in her most regal garb—satin studded with pearls, opals, and sapphires. She crowns you with diamonds and fiery rubies. You yield to her charm and grace! You absorb her divine beauty and tranquillity. You emerge buoyant with love and humility!

LET'S REASON

"The Sea of Love" describes the recognition of the divine within, in our own image and likeness. We now begin to feel our beauty and value, and that enables us to experience the sanctity of true and eternal love. This movement corresponds to the fourth chakra, the heart chakra. The color is green, the cool color of love and healing.

As humans, we see in our gods omnipotence and perfection, mirroring our true potential. As women, we presently have no such mirrors of our divine potential. For women of the African diaspora, God is not our gender and not our race. We are out of balance in perceiving this potential, because we have only experienced masculine images of divinity. We need to revitalize the feminine symbols, so that we can come to the *neutral* experience of the life-force that is necessary for healing.

One of my clients, a very brilliant health professional student struggling with depression and a very low sense of her own worth, remarked in a session that she could see the need to have black images of Jesus, but could never tolerate a Savior being depicted as a woman. I have also observed that African-descended women have a very hard time visualizing themselves as perfect beings. When I have taken my clients through visualization exercises of perfection within, white men offer the least resistance. African American women resist the most. It is a struggle for us to give ourselves permission to let go of the deeply ingrained feeling that we are sinful descendants of Ham.

Until the advent of Judaism, Christianity, and Islam, most ancient cultures paid homage and divine respect to the feminine energy, the life-force of creation, symbolized as the Great Mother or Goddess. She is the Egyptian Isis, the Yoruban Yemaya, the pre-Hellenic Gaia and the Greek Demeter, the Hopi Spider Woman, and the Chinese Nü-Kwa. One can only speculate that it is the envy and fear of her power that led to her denigration in the patriarchal religions that now dominate the world.

Unknown to Billie Jean and myself, at about the same time that we created our goddess image in *Soul Quest,* Malidome Some described in his book *Of Water and the Spirit* a similar goddess that he encountered in his initiation process: "My body felt like it was floating, as if it were a small child being lulled by a nurturing presence that was trying to calm me by singing soothing lullabies and rocking me rhythmically. I felt as if I were floating weightless in a small body of water. My eyes were locked on to the veil, and the feeling of being drawn toward her increased. For a moment I was overcome with shyness, uneasiness and a feeling of inappropriateness and I had to lower my eyes. When I looked again, she had lifted her face, revealing an unearthly face. She was green, light green. Even her eyes were green. . . . Never before had I felt so much love. . . . The sensation of embracing her body blew my body into countless pieces."

In beginning the search for the true self, we need

to internalize images of our God-self. No, African-descended woman, you are not sinning, not being a heretic, when you see God in yourself. Many of my clients feel that it is blasphemy to say, "I am God," to truly feel God in themselves. Recall being told not to take the Lord's name in vain. Imagine the difficulty assuming it for ourselves.

The following Self-Discovery Exercises encourage you to begin the process of reclaiming your true inner value and beauty. They ask you to ponder what you experience as good within you. No, you are not being narcissistic when you pay homage to the beauty of your soul. Narcissus was admiring the reflection of his physical body and face, not his inner self.

SELF-DISCOVERY EXERCISES

23.

What I love most about myself is . . .

The aspect of myself that comes closest to
    perfection is . . .

24.

I experience my higher self (higher power,
    god within) as . . .

RELEASING EXERCISE NO. 6

This allows you to mirror your inner beauty on the out-side, to radiate it outward.

Throw a party for your closest women friends. Let "The Joy of Being Alive" be the theme. Invite everyone to dress in her most stunning attire. Play your favorite music and serve your favorite food. Allow yourself to become a part of the glamour and radiance around you. As you interact with others, do so with warmth. Say only positive things in your conversations.
    Doing this exercise makes me

a. feel . . .

b. think . . .

Beauty is life when life unveils her holy face.
—Kahlil Gibran

MOVEMENT 7

SONGS UP HIGH

US women of the diaspora
Yes, come rejoice,
Drown out our worries
With constant chatter.
We cannot hear
Our celestial voice
Or any one else's
For that matter.

Silence! Tune into your wavelength
Listen to your aria full-strength.

IMAGINE

Evening has come to your paradise isle. Dusk invites you to attend the last picture show, held nightly at the court high above Blue River Bay.

The sky, dressed in her royal blue silk robes, has offered her stage to the vanishing light as she gives birth to the dark, mysterious night.

Jubilantly you climb to the top of the hill, seeking the front row for the celebration of time ever-changing.

The trumpets sound once more. The mighty archangel's lure heralds the golden chariots, come to take the sun to her other home across the sky.

Triumphantly she takes one last bow, spraying final good-bye smiles and kisses, from lips still red, but now faintly painted.

The cherubs-in-waiting, swathed in lively blue shrouds, lay her head upon the puffy, white clouds, and cover her with her blanket, the warm blue sky.

From your bluff side seat, you throw her one parting kiss. Majestic, she lies in her cradle! You applaud the celestial spectacle. The curtains begin to close. Slowly she shuts her weary eyes.

You join the birds as they chant their lullaby high above. You open your voice to the songs of the sages echoing into the river down below.

You let the sacred sounds vibrate through you: Life begins in me, Life maintains in me, Life ends in me.

LET'S REASON

"Songs Up High" is about opening up and expressing ourselves honestly, speaking from our hearts. To be honest with others, we first have to be honest with ourselves. We need to know our divine truths so that we can develop more clarity about how we think and feel. This movement corresponds to the fifth chakra, located in the area of the throat. This is the center of communication, self-expression, and inner peace. This chakra vibrates to the cool color blue, that of the dusky evening sky.

How often we find ourselves afraid to speak our minds. A coping mechanism of oppressed people is self-concealment. The less the oppressors know about us, the more difficult it is for them to develop strategies to hurt us. One of the psychic survival strategies employed during slavery was to not let Massa know what we were thinking or feeling. By our silence, we gave him less to fuel the fires of aggression. How many times were we told not to open our mouths during interactions with authority figures—police, school principal, landlord—for it could get us into trouble? The more we have had to internalize this deceit, necessary for our survival, the more we have deceived ourselves. We no longer know the truth of who we are. It is only when we become comfortable with ourselves, when we accept our truths as best we know them, that we are able to assert ourselves confidently with others.

The road back to the truth is love. Love gives us the power and confidence to face the reality of that which is and isn't. It is fear that makes us distort. Love conquers all—most of all, fear. With the publication of the first edition of *Soul Quest,* I felt acutely vulnerable. I feared that others would not find it meaningful. I was worried that when I had to speak before an audience, I would forget what I had to say, express it incorrectly, or be unable to answer a question. I was afraid that I would be humiliated and attacked. When I realized, however, that *Soul Quest* was a work of love from my heart to my people, and that what came from my heart must be true, I stopped being afraid. Audiences were seeking the truth. They came to hear me, not to attack. They wanted to share the knowledge I had to impart. I began to view my audiences differently and became more confident in my public speaking.

It is a tremendous release for clients when they can begin to be honest with those around them. It is empowering for them to finally tell their mates, their parents, their bosses, their children, what they really think, no matter what the consequence. Often they find that the consequences are much less scary than they thought. Before they can find the truth, however, they have to begin to pay attention to their true feelings.

They have to listen to themselves.

One such client, a successful businesswoman working in her family's business, realized that all her life she had been operating under her family code: "Never let others know your business; don't let outsiders interfere." All her life she has assumed the persona of a member of "a righteous, upper-middle-class black family." She has always been extremely gregarious, "the life of the party." As a child she never told anyone of an older relative's threats of molesting her. As an adult working alongside her family, she has been unable to assert herself in business decisions. Owing to worsening depression, she sought therapy. A major struggle for her in therapy was wanting to appear in control. Her major defense mechanism had been minimization, that is, decreasing the extent of the pain she

57

felt. "We've had a little incest in our family" was how she opened up a discussion of the suicide of a family member who was molested by another family member. With time, as she began to feel nurtured, protected, and valued in her working alliance with me, she felt less of a need to be perceived as being strong. She allowed her tears to flow, to let go of the tightness in her chest that she described as "squeezing the life" out of her. She began to speak about the layers of fear and pain that she carried for so many years. Most of her pain centered around not feeling loved and protected by her distant and controlling mother.

Many African-descended women are afraid to be perceived as being out of control of their emotions. No matter how overwhelmed they feel, no matter how things are falling apart, they maintain a cheerful persona, an illusion that "everything is okay." By the time most African-descended women seek professional help, their lives have become almost unmanageable; they can barely maintain the illusion of wellness.

The following Self-Discovery Exercises challenge you to come out from under your lies, and encourage you to explore your level of assertiveness, to think about how honestly you communicate your feelings.

SELF-DISCOVERY EXERCISES

25.

The last situation in which I did not tell another person exactly what I wanted to was . . .

My feelings then were . . .

My thoughts were (the things I told myself about the situation) . . .

I actually wanted to say to the other person . . .

26.

The next time I find myself in a similar situation, I am going to . . .

RELEASING EXERCISE NO. 7

This challenges you to open up and speak. But only after you have contemplated your truths in silence.

Identify an activity that you have always secretly wished you had the courage to do (for example, recite a poem or passage or sing in public, or confront someone who has hurt you). This activity should be an honest reflection of who you think you are if you could be totally free. Visualize yourself acting out this desire now. Share this with the person whom you feel loves you the most. What was the response?

Doing this exercise makes me

a. feel . . .

b. think . . .

Only when you drink from the river of silence shall you indeed sing.
—Kahlil Gibran

MOVEMENT 8

THE CRYSTAL TEMPLE BY THE RIVER

US women of the diaspora
Yes, nearly blinded by our rut,
See with both eyes half shut.
Blocking the pain of yesteryears,
Viewing only what's happening here.

Open wide your third eye sublime,
Enter the temple of never-ending time.

IMAGINE

It is the magic moment, twilight. Sister stars are smiling. Mother moon is full, ripe, and beaming light kisses. An enchanted boat, hovering near, offers you passage beneath the amethyst sky, to a secret shrine.

You wind your way up the Blue River. You notice a crystal temple along her banks, and stop to offer thanks. As you sprinkle your libations upon the waters, you slip into a timeless, spaceless realm.

You enter and lie at the temple's purple altar. You inhale the sweet violas' essence, mixed with burning frankincense. Vestal maidens with golden chains around their waists, and silver bells on their toes, remove your dusty, worn-out clothes. They massage you all over with sandalwood. They drape you in light purple silk and feed you sweet milk and honey. Crowning you with garlands of irises, they proclaim you grand high priestess. You anoint their heads with lavender oil, and rub them all over with sacred myrrh. You mix their sacred flow with lilacs, as offering for the waiting earth.

You chant up high to the goddess of fertile splendor:

Bless us, the bearers of
The eternal fruits of life.
Open all our senses
To then, now, and always.

LET'S REASON

"The Crystal Temple by the River" describes listening to and trusting our inner voice, our intuition. This movement helps us to recognize our wiser, intuitive self, which knows the true meaning of our lives. It corresponds to the sixth chakra, the third-eye chakra, the home of the pineal gland, the center of our perceptual palace. The color is blue-violet.

Most of us experience ourselves and our world only in tangible terms—that which we hear, see, smell, touch, and taste. We block out the possibility of everything else beyond this realm. In earlier times we probably would have had a hard time believing that the world was round. We must remember, however, that the universe is a nonlinear, chaotic, and dynamic system. It is extremely sensitive, at times responding unpredictably to feedback. We cannot, therefore, reduce our understanding of it to solely linear, logical, and pre-dictable thinking. Those of us who open up to this expanded sensory experience of our universe, open up to intuition.

I am no longer puzzled by the many twists and turns in my life that led to my decision to do my residency training in psychiatry, as opposed to internal medicine. It seemed only natural that I would specialize in the latter. During my clinical rotations in medical school I got an A in internal medicine and a C-plus in psychiatry. I see now that if I had stayed in internal medicine, I would perhaps have become stuck in the physical self. Psychiatry made it easier for me to leap to the spirit, especially after I discovered the works of Carl Jung and left behind the more traditional Freudian approach. Given that much of Jung's knowledge came from his studies of Eastern philosophies, and some of his experiences while traveling in Africa, it was very easy for me to jump from Jung to the mystical.

From age three to five, my oldest daughter twice reported having lived previous lives. In our present society, the ability to remember past lives is too often dismissed or even ridiculed, even by our parents. Her spontaneity in slipping into another time zone made a believer out of me.

We, the people of the African diaspora, have had our intuitive spirit driven out of us. It was important to the oppressors that we be so exorcised, because intuitiveness could make us unruly. People who are in touch with their intuition liberate themselves from simple cause-and-effect reasoning, from black-and-white reductionist thinking. It is easier to control a people who believe only in what's happening here and now. Further, if people block their intuitive perceptions, it is easier for the oppressors to get them to follow a prescribed scripture of redemption. Many of us have held on to our multisensory intuitiveness through our religions and spiritual practices, such as Obeah, Voudun, and Shango.

No matter how it has been disguised, we have always had a special relationship with the spirits of our ancestors. When we are given permission to speak of such things, it is fascinating to hear how many of us have had real experiences of communicating with spirits—of knowing, for example, that someone has just died, or of having someone recently deceased appear to us. Those of us from the Caribbean or Louisiana seem to be more honest in admitting these experiences. A client of mine recalled how, at the hour of her mother's death, her dead father appeared to her and told her that he had come to take his wife. Two of her mother's friends called within the hour to tell her that her mother must have just died,

because she had appeared to them, telling of her death. (The day following this session, my father-in-law passed away. I felt strongly that my client had primed me for this event.) A friend recalled how, during a flight, she had a sensation of something grabbing her. She panicked. A close aunt appeared in her thoughts, and she prayed that her aunt would not die. When she called home later, she found out that her aunt had died at just about the time she had panicked.

Many African-descended women have highly developed modalities of extrasensory perception. Many of us have felt certain outcomes before they occurred. Too often, however, because of a lack of trust in such feelings, we do not use these abilities to help in our decision-making. I have known women who dreamed of meeting their mates before they actually did. I have also known women who had premonitions of their mates' infidelity. They had no concrete evidence, just a feeling. A client of mine recalled how, upon introducing a friend to her husband, she had a sinking feeling that they were going to have a relationship; they are now married. Have you ever gone on a job interview and known you were going to get the job even before the interview occurred, just had that feeling from the "vibes" around you? Many of us can testify to having seen the predictions of psychics and readers actually come to pass.

It is our connection to intuition that keeps many of

us reading horoscopes, no matter how superficial this might be. Birth signs are very important to many African-descended women. We truly believe that celestial occurrences at the time of our birth are important determinants of our personality traits.

Many of our grandparents had special powers of communication with plants and animals. Some of us have had grandmothers who could talk to the trees. In times of illness they could always find the exact herb, "bush," to heal us. They couldn't explain how it worked; they just knew that it did. Some of us have had grandfathers who spoke to their horses and donkeys and could at times tell what was wrong with them when they weren't "acting right." Some of us from the Caribbean know that the calf, "rolling calf," can bring us messages from the grave. We heard their chains when our elders summoned their presence.

Our music and dance traditions have kept us connected outside of and beyond our physical selves. Reggae, jazz, blues, and rap communicate among all our global souls. No matter where we are from, the Caribbean, the U.S.A., or Latin America, no matter what colonial language we speak, we all understand the messages of rhythm. We must not forget that the slaves all knew the meaning of the blowing of the "Abeng."

By beginning to reclaim our cultural intuitiveness, we also regain the personal intuition. The Self-Discovery Exercises below are designed to increase your awareness of those unexplainable but real experiences of extrasensory perceptions that you have had, and the meaningful "coincidences" that have occurred in your life. If you pay better attention to them, you will begin to receive guidance about the meaning of your life, that special purpose and mission that you are here to accomplish.

SELF-DISCOVERY EXERCISES

27.

The last time I met someone with whom I felt an instant bond (as if I had known the person all my life) was . . .

The last time I thought about someone and I heard from or about that person very shortly thereafter was . . .

The last time I visited a place and had a feeling I had been there before was . . .

28.

If it is possible to have lived before, I think I would have been . . .

29.

If it is possible to live again, I would like to come back as . . .

RELEASING EXERCISE NO. 8

This challenges you to imagine the possibilities if only you would open up to your multisensory self.

Make a list of times you wish you had done what your first feelings told you to, "if only I had followed my mind!"

Doing this exercise makes me

a. feel . . .

b. think . . .

And yet the timeless in you is aware of life's timelessness, and knows that yesterday is but today's memory and tomorrow is today's dream.
—Kahlil Gibran

MOVEMENT 9

SOUL FLIGHT

US women of the diaspora,
Sorrow-filled dears,
Have clipped our wings
With the salt of our tears.
Mourning cords long ago left behind,
Which now we are desperate to find.

Wipe those tears! They must stop!
If we are to reach the mountaintop!

IMAGINE

Midnight has come to your temple of gold. It is time to rest your fulfilled soul. You drift into blissful sleep, silvery white Narcissus as pillow. Your soul is full, light and feathery as willow.

Your dreams are pierced with a vibrant kiss. You awaken to the Moon Goddess, calling out to you, her newly found Sister, "Come visit in my garden! Eve has finally taken pardon. Eden can now be retaken."

She leads you to a gazebo laden with fragrant vines. You lather in the juice of the sweet night jasmines. You sip the nectar of honeysuckle, wine of the holy and divine. You wrap your soul in warm, soft light, slipping deep into night. Your body begins to float aside. You glide naked into liquid flight.

As the owls serenade you with their silver flutes, you ascend higher and higher. You hop on a silver moonbeam spiraling in her sacred stream. Spinning faster than her light, you enter the land beyond the night.

Suddenly, all of self comes alight. All pathways of being become bright. Duality merges, opposites unite. A kaleidoscope of ageless visions moves forward and backward in one. Timeless and spaceless, you meet the sky. Your slave lady rejoins her liberty; dark and light together in unity.

You claim yourself eternal!

LET'S REASON

"Soul Flight" describes the journey into our eternal self. It challenges us to experience the spirit unfolding in our daily, ordinary existence and not wait until the next religious gathering. This movement corresponds to the seventh chakra, the crown chakra. It represents spiritual healing, alignment, and transcendence of the soul. The color is pale lavender or pink.

How do we find spirituality in the present? By seeing the life-force manifested in all that surrounds us and approaching each day with humility and reverence. By trusting that, as part of the divine life plan, the Great Mother Earth will take care of us. However, we must clear out the excess baggage, the clutter that blocks our ability to see and hear our spirit messages. This means simplifying our lives, slowing down and finding quietude at some point each day. It's hard for inspiration to find us when we are constantly zigzagging our way through life. By being ready to feel spirit working, we will be able to move through the windows that it opens.

During a period of upheaval in my life, a social-worker colleague suggested that I repeat the mantra *Om Namah Shivaya*. I was somewhat taken aback that my cloak of being okay was becoming translucent; however, knowing the reality of the restlessness I was feeling inside, I thought I would give it a try. That very weekend, her spiritual leader was going to be in town, visiting the temple. I accepted her invitation to join the early-morning meditation hour. As I pulled up to the temple, worrying that I'd be late, and was fumbling with my car keys, rushing to get inside, the guru walked by my car. She looked into my eyes. Her eyes were full of life and joy. I felt they told me to slow down. In one quick and simple moment, my whole life changed. The meaningless quest for material fulfillment ended. My meaningful journey for peace and solace began. Now: *My children are sacred to me. My spouse is sacred to me. My family and friends are sacred to me. The stranger is sacred to me. The plants and the animals are sacred to me. My job and co-workers are sacred to me.*

We must not, however, confuse spirituality with laziness and giving up. The spiritual path is not to sit back and wait for the life-force to move us. The spiritual path is to do life in concert with all the universal forces that surround us. All that spirituality asks of us is that we give up the narcissism of wanting to control the paths of those forces we cannot control—other people and the natural order of nature. Spirituality insists that we take control of what we can—ourselves. We are responsible for our sadness, even if it is caused by what others have done to us. My clients who have found the most fulfilling relationships are those who stopped looking for others to make them happy and began doing so for themselves. Others became attracted to the joy that they exuded.

We are able to bring reverence into our lives when we bring our constructs of the divine—our Jesus, our Buddha, or Muhammad, our Isis, our Shango—within ourselves, when we can say, "I am God manifest in me," and act accordingly. A client of mine had been at war with a co-worker known throughout the community as a cold and domineering woman. They were having difficulties completing projects because this woman would sabotage plans she did not agree with. One day the co-worker turned up at a presentation that my client was making. My client became very anxious and upset because she felt that this woman's presence spoiled the intimacy of the presentation she was giving. Feeling trapped, my client went within herself and asked to move to a higher level and be loving. When her co-worker raised her hand to respond to a question that my client asked of the audience, my client felt sure that her response was going to be antagonistic. To her surprise, her co-worker revealed a very soft and vulnerable side in support of my client's position. Since this interaction, my client has approached all communications with this co-worker through connecting with the divine in both their spirits. The war is now over; there is a truce as they redefine their strategies to get to the common goal they both have always shared.

When we see the spiritual side of every situation, we become much less judgmental and rigid; we construct fewer boundaries and become humble in our truths. We no longer feel a need to ostracize or convert those who have differing beliefs. We respect the divine in them too. The ancient philosophies teach that attainment of spiritual enlightenment comes with uniting the duality and opposites in our lives; experiencing them as complements to each other. In ancient Egypt, this was symbolized by the *ankh,* the sign of the unity of masculine and feminine images; in Chinese Taoist philosophy it is represented by the balance of yin and yang.

We women of the diaspora are the salvation of tomorrow. No one else has the potential for living life in all its poles. To do so, we must slip out from under the slave women of the past.

Good-bye, slave ladies; we have done you well. Welcome the new empresses of our land.

SELF-DISCOVERY EXERCISE

This Self-Discovery Exercise is meant to be incorporated into your daily routine, to become part of your life plan to listen to the God within you, giving you direction.

30. FOCUSED RELAXATION

Find a quiet space at home and spend at least thirty minutes alone there each day. Allow very little peripheral stimuli in this space, except soft music, candles, or incense if you desire.

Close your eyes and center your thoughts on a burning flame. As your thoughts try to fan out, try to bring them back to the central theme. When you feel sufficiently centered, allow your thoughts to wander wherever they choose. Only watch them, do not follow them.

As I focus on my breathing, as I relax my muscles, as I allow my body to develop a sensation of floating upon a cloud, the following comes to mind . . .

RELEASING EXERCISE NO. 9

This should also become a lifetime ritual. By creating a sacred space in your home, you are positively affirming and honoring your God-self, the true self.

Create an altar in your favorite room, using items of deep meaning to you, such as a favorite picture, book, flower, or plant. Each morning and/or night, spend at least five minutes before your altar, focused only on your breath. At least once a month, spend at least thirty minutes at the altar listening to your favorite music. This is your sacred space.

Doing this exercise makes me:

a. feel . . .

b. think . . .

(Come back and complete this section again after
   three months of practice.)

The soul unfolds itself like a lotus of countless petals.
—Kahlil Gibran

EPILOGUE

SOUL-UPRISING

US women of the diaspora
Have now claimed our souls' divine fate.
Bursting through the chains of the past
Floating high above the pearly gate.
Victory at last! Peace at last!
Rejoice with us, come join our heavenly choir
Guaranteed to set your heart afire.

SONG FOR OUR CHILDREN

On the occasion of your blessed birth
Let me give thanks for another jewel
Come to shine bright upon this earth.
Let me tenderly caress your colored skin.
Joseph, in his coat so bright,
Is sure to be your kin.
Oh, sacred and noble child,
Let me kiss your full, luscious lips
So noble a cup from which to sip
Your soul's sweet nectar as it drips.

Let me play in your tightly locked curls
From which life's mysteries unfurl.
Precious lamb, darkly stained Tahitian pearl.

SONG FOR OUR LOVERS

With you my love has no desire
but to feel our hearts unite
In the splendor of a liquid, moonlit night.
With you my love has no desire
but to sip together the sweet juices
Dripping from the lips of the divine muses.

With you my love has no desire

but to inhale the lingering perfume

Of our bodies stripped bare in a rose-filled room.

With you my love has no desire

but to hear the melodious explosion

As our souls rock in constant motion.

With you my love has no desire

but for our eyes in unison to see

Shared visions of blessed eternity.

With you my love has no desire other than to be.

SONG FOR OUR PEOPLE

It feels so good to be with my people,

To be cradled in bosoms fortified with chains of
*   endurance,*

To be suckled at breasts from which eternal life
*   flows,*

To look into eyes and see the wisdom and grace
*   of God.*

Oh! To be loved

And touched by my people

Is to enter the splendor

Of the garden of forever.

Rise up and embrace your true power,

Noble souls of the diaspora.

L ET'S REASON

SUMMATION OF THE NINE MOVEMENTS OF
ENLIGHTENMENT

1. Review past significant sociocultural and autobiographical events, so that you might understand and release the hurt from the negative forces in your life.

2. Open up to the complementary shadow of your pain—the pleasure of being alive.

3. Connect with the infinite power that resides in nature.

4. Celebrate the body—the beautiful temple of your soul.

5. Forgive self and others for old hurts.

6. Open to love—connect with your inner God-self.

7. Speak honestly from your heart—the joy of living the truth.

8. Trust your intuition, be guided by your inner voice.

9. Tune into and honor the sacred spirit ever present in you.

During the 1950s and 1960s we attempted to gain political power; in the 1970s, 1980s, and 1990s we have been struggling for economic equity. As we move into the twenty-first century, the Age of Aquarius, the struggle is for spiritual enlightenment. Science must become balanced with the spirit in order that we not become annihilated by our destructive technological advancements. Who better than we of the African diaspora to lead this movement? We still carry the spirit in our ancestral collective while we exist in this present-day material world. We are the bridge.

Luckily, no one can block your spiritual path but you yourself. No laws, no courts. You are in control. Spiritual development is between you and the universe. Those who would oppose you cannot draw up coun-

terstrategies, because the path is invisible. Who will be our leaders? Who will heed the peaceful battle call?

Soul Quest is meant to educate, to elicit from you that which is in you; for in your soul resides its infinite wisdom. It does not offer a recipe for happiness, just suggestions for ingredients. To the ancient Egyptians, education was seen as the liberation of the soul. *Soul Quest* challenges you to free your soul and become the captain of your own ship, the one that will lead to your exodus from captivity. As Bob Marley wrote,

> *Exodus, movement of Jah people*
> *Open your eyes and look within*
> *Are you satisfied with the life you're living*
> *We know where we are going*
> *We know where we are from*
> *We're leaving Babylon*
> *We're going to our father's (mother's) land.*
> *Exodus, movement of Jah people*

Soul Quest is a bridge between Eastern and Western philosophies, a blend of old and new. On personal and cultural frameworks, *Soul Quest* aims to build meaningful constructs of the past and integrate and expand them into frontiers of the New Age. Now that you have finished the *Soul Quest* journey, you will need to move into the driver's seat. Where are you headed? Some of you may want to go to Africa, Tibet, Mecca, or Jerusalem. But most will want to journey inward, close to home. And what will you find? Do you have a map?

The course will seem tortuous at times, as if you were spinning your wheels and getting nowhere. Do not worry. This is a sign that you are on the right path. It is not linear, as you would expect. DNA, the building block of life, is helical; it is wrapped around and upon itself. The chakras are spiral in form; they circle out, then back on themselves, then circle out again. Just as your fingerprints are uniquely yours, so is your journey. In order to have meaning, your journey will have to come from your person. To begin to draw your map, start with the final destination and work your way backwards. Identify stops along the way, for rest and refueling. What do you need to take along to be prepared? If you get lost, if you make a wrong turn, do not be afraid to ask for help to get back on course. An infant learning to walk does not stop trying the first time she falls down. She stands up and tries again.

Come back to *Soul Quest* often, to check in, to see how far you've gone. However, if you find you are not going anywhere after several attempts, it probably means that you need some additional help in resolving past and present issues, "the here and now." If you are currently experiencing persistent feelings of sadness, anger, and/or fearfulness, you must seek more structured help. For some, support groups or sisterhood groups may be all that is needed. The National Black Women's Health Project is an excellent resource, as are twelve-step programs such as Alcoholics Anonymous.

For those who feel out of control, or have "bad nerves" or suicidal urges, please seek professional help with a social worker, psychiatrist, psychologist, or substance-abuse counselor. You may be feeling out of control because you are trying so hard to be *in* control. Disturbances of your sleep and/or appetite pattern, or persistent negative thoughts about yourself or others, may be additional signs that you are currently overwhelmed and broken down by your emotions. You will need intensive restructuring by someone who is properly trained to help you fit the pieces together. If friends and family whom you have previously trusted are recommending that you seek help, listen to them. Their interference is motivated by love. Wouldn't you want happiness for someone you loved, too?

Soul Quest models the enrichment that can be attained when spirit is integrated into mind/body wellness. Approaches to health for African-descended peoples cannot ignore spirit. It is spirit that has been our companion and guide when our human brothers, our oppressors, have failed us and taken us to our graves. It is spirit that will lead us to the green pastures of global peace and individual health. We can no longer afford to be fooled into thinking that religiosity and spirituality are the same. Truly to have spirit, we must bring the life-force back home to dwell always within ourselves and see God manifest in everyone else. With spirit, we will end the war with self and others. We will revere all our bodies and minds as the earth-temple of God.

RELEASING EXERCISE NO. 10 (SELF-MAINTENANCE)

That which I am doing daily to maintain my balance and contentment today and each day henceforth is . . .

My tune-up plan, to be done at regular intervals, is . . .

If in the twilight of memory we should meet once more, we shall speak again together and you shall sing to me a deeper song.
—Kahlil Gibran

RESOURCES

You may contact the following organizations to seek information regarding referrals for additional support:

American Psychiatric Association
1400 K Street, N.W., Washington, DC 20005
202-682-6000

American Psychological Association
750 First Street, N.E., Washington, DC 20002
800-374-2721

Association of Black Psychologists
P.O. Box 55999, Washington, DC 20040-5999
202-722-0808

Black Psychiatrists of America
P.O. Box 1758, North Little Rock, AR 72115
501-661-1202, ext. 4029

CDC National HIV/AIDS Hotline
800-342 2437

Center for the Prevention of Sexual and Domestic Violence
1914 N. 34th Street, #105, Seattle, WA 98103
206-634-1903

Center for Substance Abuse Treatment– National Drug Hotline
11426-28 Rockville Pike, #410, Rockville, MD 20852
800-662-4357

National Association of Black Social Workers
8436 West McNichols Avenue, Detroit, MI 48221
313-862-6700

National Association of People with AIDS
1413 K Street, N.W., #700, Washington, DC 20005
202-898-0414

National Association of Social Workers
750 First Street, N.E., #700, Washington, DC 20002
800-638-8799

National Black Women's Health Project
1237 Ralph David Abernathy Boulevard
Atlanta, GA 30310
404-758-9590

National Council of Negro Women
1001 G Street, N.W., #800, Washington, DC 20001
202-628-0015

National Institute of Mental Health
1021 Prince Street, Alexandria, VA 22314
800-969-6642

National Medical Association
1012 10th Street, N.W., Washington, DC 20001
202-347-1895

Survivors of Incest Anonymous
P.O. Box 21817, Baltimore, MD 21222
410-282-3400

Victims' Services Incest Hotline
212-227-3000

FURTHER READING

ben-Jochannan, Yosef A. A. *They All Look Alike! All?!* New York: self-published.

Chopra, Deepak. *Ageless Body, Timeless Mind*. New York: Crown Publishers, 1993.

Diop, Cheikh Anta. *The African Origins of Civilization*. Westport, Conn.: Lawrence Hill & Co., 1974.

Gibran, Kahlil. *The Prophet*. New York: Alfred A. Knopf, 1923.

James, George G. M. *Stolen Legacy*. San Francisco: Julian Richardson Associates, 1976.

Leadbetter, C. W. *The Chakras*. Wheaton, Ill.: Theosophical Publishing House, 1985.

Leeson, Robert. *The Cimaroons*. Glasgow: William Collins and Son, 1978.

Redfield, James. *The Celestine Prophecy*. New York: Warner Books, 1994.

Silko, Leslie Marmon. *Almanac of the Dead*. New York: Simon and Schuster, 1991.

Some, Malidome Patrice. *Of Water and the Spirit*. New York: G. P. Putnam's Sons, 1994.

Stein, Diane. *The Women's Spirituality Book*. St. Paul: Llewellyn Publications, 1987.

Tesh, Luisah. *Carnival of the Spirit*. San Francisco: HarperCollins, 1994.

Van Sertima, Ivan, ed. *Nile Valley Civilizations*. New Brunswick, N.J.: Journal of African Civilizations, 1985.

Vanzant, Iyanla. *The Value in the Valley*. New York: Simon and Schuster, 1995.

Villarosa, Linda, ed. *Body and Soul*. New York: Harper Perennial, 1994.

Welsing, Frances Cress. *The Isis Papers*. Chicago: Third World Press, 1991.

Wolf, Fred Alan. *The Eagle's Quest*. New York: Simon and Schuster, 1991.

Zukav, Gary. *The Seat of the Soul*. New York: Simon and Schuster, 1989.

INDEX

Ageless Body, Timeless Mind
  (Chopra), 21
Birth signs, 64
Body, 8, 35, 37, 38

Chakras, 6, 75. *See also specific chakras*
Children, 13–14, 43
Chopra, Deepak, 21
Codependency, 29
Communication, 56, 58–59
Concealment, 56
Conflict, 12
Control, 12, 75
Crown chakra, 6, 68

Death, 63
Divinity, 50–52, 69, 70

Ego, 12–13, 37
Eternal self, 68
Extrasensory perception, 63

Fear, 21, 22, 57, 58
Forgiveness, 42, 45–47

Gestalt theory, 20
Gibran, Kahlil, 17, 25, 31, 38, 47,
  53, 59, 65, 71, 76

Healing, 50
Heart chakra, 6, 50
HIV infection, 36
Homosexuality, 36
Honesty, 56, 57

Intuition, 62–64

Journal-keeping, 8
Joy, 25
Jung, Carl, 62

Love, 50, 57

Malcolm X, 13
Marley, Bob, 9, 13, 25, 74
Masturbation, 36–37
McMillan, Terry, 29
Middle Passage, 14
Mosi Oi Tunya (Victoria Falls), 21, 29
Mothers, 42-45

Nature, 20, 28, 29, 31

Of Water and the Spirit (Some), 51

Pain, 12, 17, 21, 57–58
Personal relationships, 29, 36,
  43–44, 45

Physical appearance, 35–36
Pleasure zones, 23

Rape, 34–35
Relationships. *See* Personal relationships
Relaxation, 71
Religion. *See* Divinity; Spirituality
Root chakra, 6, 28

Self-discovery exercises, 16–17, 24, 30,
  38, 47, 53, 59, 65, 71
Self-reliance, 13
Sex, 34–35, 37
Slavery, 14, 28, 34, 56
Solar plexus (umbilical) chakra, 6, 42
Some, Malidome, 51
Soul, 74
Spirituality, 68–71, 74, 75–76
Splenic chakra, 6, 34
Stress response, 21

Third-eye (brow) chakra, 6, 62
Throat chakra, 6, 56

Waiting to Exhale (McMillan), 29

Zambezi River, 13, 21
Zimbabwe, 13, 21, 34, 43

ABOUT THE AUTHOR

Denese Shervington, M.D., M.P.H., is a Clinical Professor of Psychiatry at Louisiana State University School of Medicine. Jamaican-born Dr. Shervington is a graduate of New York University School of Medicine; she completed her residency in psychiatry at the University of California San Francisco. She received a master's degree in Public Health in International Studies from Tulane University School of Public Health and Tropical Medicine. She is certified by the American Board of Psychiatry and Neurology.

Dr. Shervington's area of professional interest and focus is women's reproductive and mental health.

 Dr. Shervington practices yoga and meditation. She is interested in the holistic integration of ancient and modern approaches to personal growth and wellness. Together with Dr. Pace, she conducts seminars and retreats on mind-body-spirit healing and leadership development.

THE ILLUSTRATOR

Billie Jean Pace, M.D., is a gynecologist in private practice in Altamonte Springs, Florida. Dr. Pace received her M.D. degree from Howard University School of Medicine in Washington, D.C. She completed her internship and residency training in obstetrics and gynecology at Martin Luther King Jr. General Hospital in Los Angeles, California.

Dr. Pace's years of experience in women's health have focused on the whole person, and embrace the emotional and spiritual aspects of wellness along with the physical. She supports a holistic and preventive approach to health and well-being. In addition to her own life-long interest in the visual arts, as represented by the

 eleven airbrush illustrations in this book, Dr. Pace finds personal balance as a student of yoga.